Waves Rough and Smooth
&
the Deep Blue Sea

Edward Conklin Ph.D.

ISBN: 978-0-9906457-1-9

Acknowledgement

I acknowledge and thank family, friends, teacher, intimate loves, and muse, who without their profound presence, these poems could not have been written.

Published works by Edward Conklin Ph.D.

Psychology of God and the Soul. (2016). Amazon Kindle and CreateSpace.

Meditations on God and the Soul. (2015). Amazon Kindle and CreateSpace.

A Brief Guide to God and the Soul. (2015). Amazon Kindle and CreateSpace.

In the Beginning: A New Theory of the First Religion. (2014). Amazon Kindle and CreateSpace.

Cosmos, God, and Soul. (2014). Amazon Kindle and CreateSpace.

From Tool-maker to God Maker. (2014). Amazon Kindle and CreateSpace.

Waves Rough and Smooth & the Deep Blue Sea. (2014). Amazon Kindle and CreateSpace.

Getting Back Into the Garden of Eden. (1998). University Press of America.

Across the flowered meadow, beneath sun-dappled trees,
Enchanting colored wings flutter by on a gentle breeze.

Brightly colored flowers for butterflies and bees,
For human beings each other to please.

To and fro flits a butterfly in flight,
Seeking beauty and sweetness there to alight.

Winging and gliding upon the transparent air,
In loving communion a butterfly pair.

Two butterflies floating, swirling, each other inviting,
In intimate and amorous touches delighting.

Gently appearing in the shimmering light,
An iridescent butterfly in transcendent flight.

Through an invisible air, space, and time,
On gossamer wings float a butterfly sublime.

Among lovely petals bees hover around,
Coming and going when nectar is found.

Weeds all grow from a common ground,
But here and there a flower is found.

Delicate flowers open to sun and dew,
Wanting to touch and be touched too.

"You must now learn to love", you said to me,
I said, that is the hard part,
And you answered, "A bud must open into a flower,"
Now the petals slowly unfold.

Often returns, sweet memory of that day,
Into your dark eyes looking, pupils dilate, aglow, opening,
Touching my heart forever with the rapture of cosmic love.

Open O' heart, portal to the infinite,
Melt and flow, forming your mystical embrace
Of sunshine and breezes.

Cosmic fire, earth, water, and air,
Forms sublime, supporting, caressing,
And commingling with me all the day and night long.

From an all pervading unseen source,
Have come the seeds of relative force,
For all that is has come to be,
As a divine function of polarity.

Round the universe, the whole is complete in parts diverse.

O' primordial One, that from which these parts have come.

Numinous ecstasy yet shame and pain of human sexuality.

Pushed out into life and pulled into death.

Living to acquire what we desire,
Working for hire until we perspire,
One day to retire and then expire.

Peaceful place of many a green and flowered plot,
Granite stones there to mark the spot,
Of life that once was and now is not.

All things made of wood it's quite plain to see,
Now just a skeleton part of a once living tree.

In business or politics having left not a mark,
Of life this only asked before I depart,
To utter a few plain words that touch the heart.

Keep all your money, possessions, fame, and the rest,
Enough for me delirious sweet touches of tenderness.

Into my life one day you came,
And within my heart kindled a glowing flame;

Body and mind do often yearn,
In the consuming fire of love to burn.

From outside, often seen to be average, busy, unconcerned,
But inside, there silent yet all the while present,
A profound need to touch and be touched in turn.

For loving touches we do yearn, to receive and give in return.

Love is a magnetic mystery, to and from pulling you and me.

How many times must this lesson be learned?
It is the touch that matters, not to have and hold.

Often within lilts the refrain, sometimes no one is to blame,
Touches of love include both pleasure and pain.

When pulling and pushing both are put aside,
The delight of touching is revealed to the eye,
And intimately felt deep down inside.

When not intent on controlling others to be,
And not overly controlling me,
Then there is only spontaneity.

For many in life balance is lost,
With scales tipped in favor of self or another,
having or not having,
Nature or a god, here or hereafter;
Heights of joy, depths of despair, balance so fair.

Not enough or too much, the suffering of life is composed of such.

From giving we cannot refrain, giving pleasure, giving pain,
Giving for a price, giving free, giving you, giving me.

Gladly all pride and distance will I surrender,
For just a few of those touches tender.

It is not from happiness or sadness that a tear now falls,
But from surrender, sweet, sweet, unalloyed surrender.

Other saviors there have been and shall be,
But here today my savior stands before me,
Exquisite to behold, sharing glances, smiles, and love.

Perhaps someday you and I will meet, somewhere, sometime upon a
street,
Then we'll say hello without any fear, and it will feel good just to be
near.

Desires to control no longer interfere, aggression removed toward
any here,
Gone the separating force of fear, now sublime touching of all that is
near.

Concerned not so much with accomplishing but appreciating this
life profound,
What I touch and what touches me, every minute of the hour.

To open the heart, this now and again do,
From the past long ago to the present view;
First remember all that you have loved,
Muse then on all who have given love to you.

Naturally the shallow rushing babbling stream,
Enters often into a deep pool of quiet stillness.

Ever moving stream of time with swirls fast and slow,
One current all propelling in an endless cosmic flow.

In one soil rooted, plants and trees all,
Many growing lowly, plain, bent, or barren,
Others lovely, fruitful, some true and tall.

Seeing, then touching, not easy to explain,
For moments into one blending, the same,
Blissful then parting atwain; ever near yet separate awhile to remain,
From a sole cosmic force, given many and many a name.

By your invisible beauty touched deeply,
Into ecstasy moved, immersed and inspired,
As a veil of mystery is parted aside.

Surrounded by thee, formed from thee,
Laved forcefully and gently ever by thee.

Within every drop of water there does seem to be,
A desire to join and flow with others in intimacy,
Also a longing to touch and blend into an infinite sea.

Storm and quiet calm are reality,
For individual droplets in an ever changing sea;
Of undulating waves and currents part, moved determinedly.

Upon the surface no longer any rough waves surging,
Finally gentle, calm,
Into the stillness of the great sea merging.

Wanting to comprehend one cosmic force, there must be one desire,
Just as when many things are wanted, there must be many desires.

Minute and large, fast and slow,
All are relative parts of a great Cosmic Go.

Gently now, after much peering, musing,
The knot of existence delicately untying.

Sometimes slowly or abruptly, to the vision surrendering,
The opposites transcending, blissful equality touching.

In and among daily chores, finding time enough to touch the timeless.

Ever at hand is an invisible form,
From which all that is visible has been born.

To comprehend one source there is an innate need,
But it is not a personality in which to believe,
But rather a tangible presence that can be perceived;
Those who realize this become free and blissful indeed.

One cosmic force, omnipresent, unadorned, transcendent and immanent,
Common to all without and within, yet from ordinary view hidden;
Sensitivity and meditative intuition only, reveal a triune soul within.

From one cosmic force both yours and mine,
Relative body, emotions, and thoughts sublime.

Libidinal force pervading all, present in the darkness unseen and
photons of light,
Cohering in breezes and droplets of flowing water,
Existent in the aromatic soil that brings forth plants and trees,
Indwelling every living form as amorous pangs, attraction and
affection.

Silent touches bringing awareness of thee,
Becoming like thee, delighting in rest, movement and attraction;
Often like thee emanating, entering into, joining,
Ecstatic overflowing of force divine.

From one invisible and divisible form,
All that is here has been born,
And like an unseen omnipresent source,
So this body aches with procreative force.

When there is a loss of sensitivity, due to inhibiting social
acceptability,
The usual fear of sharing intimacy, perhaps some limiting religiosity,
A few remembered pains of usury, instilled notions of egocentricity,
Include boring routine and monotony, or lust for only physicality;
Soon lost sight of is the numinous nature of human sexuality.

Silent source, beginningless and endless,
Yet the beginning and ending of all.

Unlimited expanse of an unseen source,
Silent, ever emanating one immanent force;
From it there has never been a fall,
Just a lack of sensitivity to perceive, that is all.

From separation into mystical union joined,
Yearning moments of buoyant bliss soon meet,
With an eternal calm merging replete.

Delicate droplet of dew, of cosmic currents and cycles part,
A numinous emanation from a great unseen sea,
One of many droplets from a single wave, among a cosmos of waves,
Ceaselessly appearing and disappearing upon the surface of the infinite.

Silent subtle presence, difficult to see;
One ever surrounding and immanent force,
Of mysterious movement and moments.

Remove from me now what does confine,
Ego thoughts of yours and mine,
Let us blend with each other for a time,
Intimate touches sharing of love sublime.

Now and then an irresistible invitation to intimacy,
Caressing eyes, caressing eyes, lovely, lovely, caressing eyes

Once a child's eyes revealed the secret of life,
In this world we are to look and feel;
Letting go of favor and disfavor we can breathlessly balance,
For moments touching in intimacy profound.
Beyond words to ever describe.

Feelings of rapture within now flowing,
After glimpsing a wildflower by the wayside growing,
Safe from any insensitive human mowing,
With all of its beauty naturally showing,
Upon the air sweet nectar bestowing.

Slow awakening to morning light,
Recalling mantic words of the night,
That an unknown specter did recite;
Brought soft flowing tears of delight,
And sensuous aesthetic oneness revealed to sight.

Onward human race you continue to toil,
More insensitive to each other becoming,
And the environment you daily soil.

Ever has the crowd been misinformed,
The important thing is not what is believed, what each has,
or how adorned,
But how sensitive to self, to others, and to an unseen cosmic form,
From which all that is here has been borne.

What is reported as news day after day, is just the same old fray,
Of conflict and crimes that will likely never go away.

Humans love opposition and conflict most of course,
Much more than seeing how each is a continuation,
Of a single shared cosmological force.

Thankful for food, drink, and bread,
But after these pass through and exit the body transformed,
We hold our nose and turn away in loathing and dread.

Unawake dreamers with eyes open or closed,
Mesmerized with images, somnambulantly reposed.

From the timeless endlessly emanating,
Effervescent moments of time,
Appearing and disappearing imageless orbs.

Simple morning task enjoyed of hanging up just washed clothes,
Soon dried by haloed sensuous sun and fresh air good to the nose,
That sweet scent savoring, better than any perfume or rose.

Amorous ache of force divine, within the body yours and mine.

Between soft smooth thighs yearning bare,
Glistening droplets of liquid love suspended there,
Adorning silken tendrils of honeyed hair.

Through many coarse earthen grains having searched and sifted,
For only a few nuggets found to be genuine golden and gifted.

Twin vows having taken, of sensitivity and simplicity,
Few possessions wanting, frequent pausing for leisure;
Fond of musing and meditating on self, others, and forces of nature;
Finite touches intimating, to insight revealing,
Triune soul force of sex, hunger, and aggression,
Immanent in every living form.

Much more meaningful are the murmurings of nature,
Primal sounds of wind through branches and leaves,
Of lightening, thunder, rain, and flowing waters,
Than any popular mutterings about a human-like god.

Usually unseen yet unhidden,
This moment, hour, and day revealed, and clearly seen,
Beyond any doubt and appearance to the contrary,
From beginning and throughout assured;
The cosmic nativity of each and all endowed with divine force.

Meditative musing calms serene, at long last awakening as from a
dream.

Removed is ignorance that separating sin,
Comprehending the opposites from beginning to end,
Never to return again and again,
With one sole cosmic force to finally blend.

Of desire for sugared deserts now finally free,
Only sweet loving touches truly satisfy me;
Drinking no more alcohol to dizzy the brain,
Sensate moments enough this heart inflame.

Many delight at the sight of the new, but care little for sight of the
old,
Yet now and then deeply moved by seeing the aged man or woman,
Decaying tree, withering plant, or discarded trash,
And the abandoned no longer sheltering house by the side of the
road.

After transition from living to dead, what if anything will be said?
That we laughed often and sometimes cried, told the truth and occasionally lied,
Did this good and that deed bad, perhaps mentioned how much we had;
Around a gravesite at the end, a gathering of relatives and a good friend.

Silent soothing death always lingering near, sooner or later intimate touches bestowing;
Then delicate moments of change from material to ethereal,
From the finite into the infinite, here disappearing, there appearing,
In illuminated dimensions beyond arriving.

Limitless procession from an invisible form of mathematical division,
Ever parting into relative additions, and times of change multiplying,
Eventual rounding complete in subtle and sudden subtraction;
A cipher becoming, disappearing, yet continuing on in other realms.

Splashing drops of water separate to exist on their own,
Each in place glistening for a time,
Till the sun appears to silently summon a change of existence.
Slowly each spherical size shrinking from sight,
Disappearing to join an invisible air,
Soon to appear as a particle of an ethereal cloud;
To drop to earth in an endless cycle,
Ever propelled by an unseen cosmic force.

Conceived, nourished, having grown day and night in wonder,
The nest having left, unsteady, expectant, yet joyful,
Launched forth from branches of the great tree,
From the flock having learned well, communed;
Now flown free, upon currents of air drifting,
In wider circles observing, rising ever higher,
Sight, sounds, and details below less important,
Gradually the ethereal resembling, form and feathers indistinct;
Now no longer an effort gliding or ascending,
Seemingly motionless, blending,
The bird one with the invisible becoming.

When finally gone from this existence let it be said that by midpoint
in life,
These few natural things were accomplished,
That I became sensitive, took the time to touch and be touched by
others,
Responded in perfect amaze and wonder to touches and beauty of
the earth,
Through rapt meditation and opening to spontaneous clear vision,
Touched others afar in space and time;
Had revealed the luminous dimensions of the afterlife and
glimpsed apparitions
on the other side;
That most often everywhere but especially when looking up at the
stars
Of the vast night sky, thoughts ceasing, body and mind filled with
awe,
Sensed a numinous force indwelling all.

Through life with senses intimately touching, having adored all;
Adored the sight, sound, taste, and feel of existence, a pageant of aesthetic mystery from beginning to end,
Adored soil, stones, and sands of the earth,
Adored storms, rain, flowing, calm and tossing waters,
Adored the high blue sky, clouds, low lying fog, cycles of day and night, and
seasons,
Adored breathing exquisite air, caressing breezes, wind sounds and quiet stillness,
Adored the shining sun, moon, planets, and distant stars,
Adored green growing plants, flowers, trees, and the miraculous seeds and fruits thereof,
Adored animals, minute and large, any swimming, crawling,
leaping, walking, climbing, and flying,
Adored relatives, friends, strangers on the street, male and female, young and old,
Good and evil, rich and poor, equally,
Adored luminous eyes, smiles, tresses of hair, natural odor, bodily movement, magnetic attraction, and affection,
Adored enchanting sensual and electric surges of sexual union,
Adored the mystery of sleeping, dreaming, waking, talking,
laughter, and tears,
Learning, musing, and meditating long,
Adored many forms here and those in ethereal dimensions beyond,
All coming from, moved by, and returning to an all-pervading cosmic force,
Above, below, around, and within all.

While many live in the bustling and growing town of Moronville,
Many more are daily moving there, while even more
Live just outside the town limits and nearby.

I prefer to overstand rather than understand.

The uneducated and unethical are frightening.

One fine day the natural rudeness of reality set in;
The earth turns a day and night show,
Of temperatures high and low
Amid winds that calm and blow,
And waters that fall and flow;
All without a care for humans.

A sublime sight to any parched tired traveler
on a sparse desert journey,
To glimpse a drink of refreshing truth.

Ever poised in now moments, between was and will be.

The gift of health surpasses all other gifts.

Most humans are blind and love makes it worse.

Children are the continuation of a coitus.

Hooray for a day away from the fray.

Every individual is a living sacrifice,
On the temporal altar of existence.

The universe is cosmological not theological

Theology has always been a waste of time,
Always will be the blind leading the blind.

Everywhere the evil One that ever brings forth,
A cosmic force which opposes nothingness or oblivion.

Many have sought the answer to the dark secret,
Of what moves all things into, through and out of existence,
And from one dimension to another;
Yet difficult to know is that which generates all things,
Supports all things, moves all things, and is beyond all things.

Who am I but an unknown hidden within a shroud of thoughts and
words?
A child playing on the shore of a vast ocean of space and time,

Nature floats on a sea of eternal force and cosmic energy,
Ever forming, joining, separating, and ending to form again.

From one cosmic force comes relative concord and discord;
Not human-like in any way, subtle, all pervading and immanent,
One cosmic force moves all into, through and out of existence.

Droplets are brought together and dispersed via
Coursing currents and waves of an ever surging sea.

Each has a date with death, ever unknowingly,
Slowly or swiftly proceeding to that day and hour.

Life precarious day by day, on the
Unseen path to death makes its way.

Only the dearest friend death can relieve,
The harshness of life at the very end.

Near the shore of silent eternity, all noisy word arguments fade.

Seeking some partial light to cast into the narrow dark byways
of life to better see,
Each surely comes to realize the narrow confines and dim serious
limitations of their existence.

Limitless forms all a limited continuation of the unlimited.

From time to time comes a feeling of surrender,
Like a wave rising to thrill in the fall and return,
To rejoin the immense presence of the sea.

Entering meditative calm,
Where personal thoughts and feelings dissolve
Into intimate oneness with you.

A bright magnetic moon connects me with you.

No longer will I be able to innocently look at the ocean waves,
As they arise from and one by one reenter the depths;
Entering the sea reminds me of the erotic act of entering you,
And becoming one with the energy of your loving blissful form.

Hearing the sound of happiness in your voice,
And lost in the gaze of your eyes,
I become drunk with desire for you.

A dream of having arrived high above, in a great room of the future poised,
Soft nooks of darkness center within, lighted windows around,
Looking out to the sky and clouds beyond, the earth below,
Meeting, walking, gazing, footsteps echoing on hardwood floors,
In this serene museum silence,
Regarding, pondering art and each other, thoughtful musing;
Here in a future anteroom of the infinite and eternal.

I am thankful for the experience
Of being able to say many loving words to you.
I've never said them to anyone else, ever;
They are all new and only for you.
They have all come unrequested out of the
Mysterious depths of heart and mind;
For this I count myself fortunate.

Did you call today and then hang up?
Was it a brief touch of remembrance?
Dropped on the sea of eternity, the ocean of forever?
Was it a lingering memory of longing for the depths?
Of touching soul energy?
But maybe these are only my own thoughts,
With nothing to do with you,
Echoes in my head of missing you.

Come, come be with me in the depths...away from this shallow world;
I long for you... my heart is broken upon the cruel shores of this lifetime.
Without you, life is but an empty shell, a hell of forlornness;
Divine energy within longs to blend with yours, longs to break free from this confining ego,
To burst into fragments to become the infinite cosmos shared with a kiss.

Just as there is learning to acquire things,
So there is a learning to let go of them.

Wisps of smoke and smoldering embers,
Cooling remnants of a once bright and blazing fire.

Life is a construction, an instruction, and a destruction.

When all is said and done, life is a letdown,
Each can only hope to see a warm smile and share a laugh,
And fall asleep in the warm arms of a beloved;
Perhaps to struggle with dreamed images and wake in the cool morning,
To struggle again through another dreamlike day.

The true goal of life is not pursuing passing pleasures,
But the avoidance of pains that will surely come and,
That may linger longer than do fleeting enjoyments.

Learn not to return.

Both biological and psychological contagion can be fatal.

Have patience with an existence composed of parts;
Some things do not go where they should be.
And some things go where they should not be.

Each looks ahead to get what is wanted and to consider it mine,
But seldom notice that all things and situations,
Are simultaneously receding away via infinite space and time.

Now moments are often unsatisfying and vain,
The past impossible to retain,
The future most difficult to ascertain.

The environment and life is contained
In a relative container of space and time,
A continuation of the uncontained and timeless.

One day rather than consider myself to be a tributary,
A small stream or river that flows into and joins with a larger river or
lake,
I began to think of myself as a distributary,
A branch of water that flows away from a body of water and does
not rejoin it.
I became a quiet stream daily distancing myself from strong social
currents,
Flowing away from the strong social rushing river.

While walking one fall day a sudden movement seen,
A leaf spiraling free from a multicolored maple tree,
Its once robust green growing life ebbing red,
Fallen onto the soft emerald grass below
Silently growing from a ground of supportive soil.
Similarly the earth, stars, and all of life that be,
In differing dimensions silently going and growing,
All a continuation of and supported by
An unseen ground of cosmological force.

www.ingramcontent.com/pod-product-compliance
Lightning Source LLC
LaVergne TN
LVHW021548080426
835509LV00019B/2910